FOR YOUR EYES ONLY

Caution: Warning Female Readers!
This Book is Only for Women
Forty-Five Years or Older

Andrea Heitzman

Order this book online at www.trafford.com
or email orders@trafford.com

Most Trafford titles are also available at major online book retailers.

Printed in the United States of America.

ISBN: 978-1-4269-5181-7(sc)
ISBN: 978-1-4269-5182-4 (hc)
ISBN: 978-1-4269-5318-7 (e)

Library of Congress Control Number: 2011900187

Trafford rev. 05/25/2011

 www.trafford.com

North America & international
toll-free: 1 888 232 4444 (USA & Canada)
phone: 250 383 6864 ♦ fax: 812 355 4082

CONTENTS

INTRODUCTION

So, I assume that you are ready to read this book. I must recommend that if you are **under aged**, that is forty nine or less, you may not be ready to read this book. BUT if you are of strong heart and mind; go right ahead.

Let me set the purpose of this book; originally it was an idea that has been brewing in my mind for some time. I wanted to see if I get rid of some of the myths that because a woman reaches her mid forties that it is considered "old", it does not mean she cannot pursue a dream or do anything else. Some people have a tendency to make us round people fit into square boxes.

I hope you find my book entertaining. I know that I have enjoyed writing and reliving my life as a young girl. I am not quite sure if I want my friends to know that I was such a dork growing up. Keep telling yourself that. It is a little embarrassing. I know they will tease me, but it's OK.

I hope it takes you back to a time of childhood fun, growing up... maybe not really wanting to grow up, to hold onto those days of ole. I can say that my childhood was good. We didn't have to worry about being kidnapped or killed. We had fun playing outside.. pretending to ride horses. Now days, it seems many children spend their days on the computer, taking them to fight/kill dragons or bad guys. I share my good times with my students, who look at me like I lived in the dark ages. Our children's' imaginations need to be kept alive with real play, not with a remote.

You have certainly heard the song "Macho Man". Have you ever wonder why it is called Macho Man? Men have it so easy. What we women have to put up with...is truly unbelievable. I admire us. Just think..we carry those babies for nine months and three more years after that. We take care of everybody. We can multitask.

We are just amazing!

Chapter 1

Let's Get Started

Are you run downed? Do you poop out at work or shopping? Are you tired of hearing the same old statements that some doctors and friends say to you? For example, "You know " (your name_, you are at that age now…blah, blah..blah. If you were to stop for a moment and translate, it would sound like this, "Hey old lady, you know you have reached close to fifty and women who reached that age you will experience certain changes …I mean everything begins to fall down or it will fall apart, honey." "Blah,blah,blah. Girls, I KNOW you have heard this before.

Did you look around to see if the doctor or your friends were talking to someone else..not you? Yeah, right. I have been there, honey.

Girls, sisters, we are not old! We are experienced. Well, with age comes experience but it does not necessarily mean decrepit. Like fine wine…with age it gets better. I know the mirror does not lie, neither does my heart and soul. I just don't feel "old", and I am tired of others telling that I am.

I see those wrinkles, but also I see a spirit of strength and determination, but that does not seem to be the way it goes. I wonder if the movie stars have experienced these "talks". Maybe their conversations sound like, "Well, famous star, what would you like me to add or take out"? I am sixty one years old, so what? I don't feel sixty one, whatever that means. I am a Rockin Woman", or as my students refer to me as the Rockin and Roll'n teacher!

Please bear with me as I take you back in time, I am sure you won't mind traveling back to a time of just being a kid, growing up in the good old days. But.. if you prefer go ahead and take your nap, don't let me stop you.

The rest of you may begin on the journey of fond memories, of memories that bring back a feeling of delight and inner peace.

I have always been an active person for as long as I can remember. (ha! I can remember.) Like any kid, I enjoyed hanging out with my friends; most of my friends were boys. I was your typical tomboy. The games I played were rough. It would make any frilly girl upset. I enjoyed being outside playing with the boys. They would always include me in their games. To be honest, sometimes I wondered if there was anything wrong with me because I liked being a tomboy. I hated dresses and those fancy patent leather shoes. My mothers insisted I wear dresses, but I wore jeans and tennis shoes, the ones with the red dot on the back of the heel during my play time. After all, I had to wear a skirt and white blouse to school. We had uniforms. And no deceit girl would wear pants out and about, except me.

You will hear me use this phrase "in those days". Well, in those days, girls wore dresses and skirts. Pants were worn only for play. I wonder if that was a way to keep girls from having fun. Think about it.

I did not have many "girl" friends growing up. Most of my friends consisted of the neighborhood boys. I could run fast, climb trees and throw a ball just as good as any boy.

It was a great time for a kid..for me. I did not worry about getting old, or even have thoughts of my parents getting old. They were just my parents.

As you guessed it, I attended Catholic schools, only at my mom's request; and "in those days" nuns wore uniforms too. Their habits covered up most of their faces, so you could not tell if they were old. They never wore makeup; we never knew the color of their hair, or even if they had any hair. In fact, they all looked alike. The only memory I have of a nun giving away her age was when she was speaking to the class and her false teeth slipped out of her mouth. UGH! My idea of old was wearing false teeth. Many years later, I found out my mom had false teeth.

At recess, I played with the boys. The recess nun would constantly speak to me about being a "lady". This must have been the beginning of me becoming a rebel.

I guess the nun was trying to change my play habits. Get it "habits". Oh well, the girls would play hopscotch or jump rope. Sometimes the girls and the boys would play kickball. I did not mind playing a game or two.

I really never worried about my looks..like some of the other girls. I had auburn hair and blue eyes, and a few freckles on my face. My mom and I would have a "stand off" every time we would go out. She would insist I wear a dress and I preferred shorts or pants. Guess who would win? Mom. It was not fair. I had to wear a dress/uniform to school and a girly dress on Sundays to church. Do you remember the I Love Lucy show? You will see that Lucy and Ethel always wore some type of dress or skirt, rarely any pants. Actually, if you remember this show; you remember that television was seen in black and white. We did not get a TV until I was about seven years old. In the good old days, we would gather around the TV, watching the show together as a family. I wonder how many families do this now.

By the way, do you remember records? Record players? My record player was a pretty teal and white color. It played three different speeds. I took in a 33 ½ record to school to show my students what a record was. Of course, they take one look at it. "Mrs. Heitzman, that is one big CD!" It is hard for them to imagine. Then I have to explain the record player…the phonograph…victrolla? You can imagine the looks I got from my students. Although one child shared that he had seen "one" at his gram's house. At this time, I am feeling very, very, very old. Then a student always asks, "Just how old are you, Mrs. Heitzman?" I respond by using my child psychology..I ask how old do you think I am? The children ponder by looking up at the ceiling. I look up there too, suspecting the answer is written on the ceiling. One student calls out, "You are twenty eight". "OK", that sounds about right. Let's get back to me being a kid.

I enjoyed being a kid and growing up in those days. Life seemed a whole lot simpler. I remember watching my mom putting lotion on her face. When I think of this time…I can actually smell the lotion. I would lie on the bed and watch her apply one lotion, next would come the liquid foundation, although I never knew what it was called. She would pat the powder on after the foundation. Then she would take her red lipstick and place a dot on each cheek and rub it in. I would chuckle at that and wonder why in the world anyone would want to do it. Next would come the lipstick to the lips; ever so carefully she would outline her lips with the red lipstick, then smack and bite down on a tissue. I never asked why, I suppose I just accepted that this is what mothers do.

Looking through my eyes, my mom was not old; I just knew I was not going to do that "girly" stuff to my face. I could not see the purpose.

Time had passed and my brother and I were getting older. My parents decided we needed a bigger house, a place where my brother and I could have our own bedroom. I didn't quite understand the need, since my brother and I got along fine.

The new neighborhood had its share of girls and boys. I met them at the local park. It didn't take long for the boys to discover my athletic abilities. The girls on the other hand could not understand why I would want to play tackle football or any other rough sport. Now realize, I am thirteen, I am not supposed to act like a tomboy now. Most of the girls my age were into boys…like ..liking them, talking about them, and writing the boy's name all over their book covers. They would discuss who they'd marry. Getting married? Not for me.

One of my best friends was a boy. One day his parents had called my parents to see if I would like to go to the Indy 500 parade. It was no big deal to me. As far as my mother was concerned …it was a big deal. I had to wear a dress, make sure my hair was pretty, and especially make sure I acted like a "lady". Here we go again.

Some of the neighborhood girls teased me stating I was going on a date. I did not appreciate their comments or their teasing. I wonder if I was resisting growing up, what was I supposed to be acting like. Is this going to some type of life pattern? I was afraid to talk to my mom about my feelings; because my mom never talked to me about boys or the changes that lay ahead of me. Again, maybe in those days, it was not discussed.

I kept up with my love of sports by joining the local park's sport program. I loved playing softball. I was good at it. By now I had made some girl friends who loved to play too. We would get together after practice and just talk. Their talk became girl talk, which meant talking about boys and doing girly stuff, like wearing makeup to look older. Good grief! I had better things to do with my life than wanting to look older for boys.

Flash forward…by now I am entering high school. High school was a new experience for me. Yes, I still am in a Catholic school. Nuns looked the same as they did in elementary school. I wonder what their secret was.

During this time, things were happening to me..to my body. My mom mentioned I needed a training bra. What was I training for? It was a spandex strap that fitted around my chest...to do what? I preferred undershirts. What was the big deal anyway? I noticed hairs growing under my arms and on my legs...growing, in other places. Again, I never asked, nor did my mom tell me anything about these changes or the birds and the bees. I kept it all to myself. Of course, you couldn't help but notice the black hair on my legs; you could've parted it with a comb. Mom went to my dad to get permission from him in order for me to shave my legs. I must admit, my legs were getting a bit hairy, like my brother's legs. Girls didn't have hairy legs, not that I noticed girls having hairy legs. My dad agreed with a sigh. He must have realized I was embarking on the point of womanhood. You are probably stuck back on the sentence that states "mom had to get dad's permission in order to shave my legs". Remember this is back in the sixties, and in those days, in my house the father was the boss, this is how it was done.

I was a sophomore in high school when it all started up again.. changes. I was in class when I had to use the restroom because my stomach hurt so much. Luckily the nuns trusted me to go by myself. I sat on the toilet and I almost past out. I saw blood on my panties! You have no idea how I felt unless you had had the same experience. What on earth was happening to me? I couldn't remember if I had fallen or tripped or something to cause me to bleed. I tried not to panic, and there was no way was I going to tell a nun. I wasn't going to tell anyone, I was so scared. Could I be dying? I took a wad of toilet paper and placed it where it needed to be. I managed to keep my composure until I made it home. It was one of the longest days of my teen life.

Now I know why I needed my own room, a place to keep my secrets. I was going through some type of life change...but no one bothered to tell me. I was in such anguish.

After the second day of you know what- the *curse*. I decided to tell my mom. I called her into the bathroom and closed the door. I was scared and extremely nervous. I really did not know where to begin. As I spoke, the color of my mom's face turned white. She acted like she didn't hear me. I knew I was going to die. There was still so much I wanted to do in life…like grow up and have my own horse. My life was over.

My mom questioned me…did I fall? Did I sit on my bike the wrong way? Say, what kind of question is that? The more questions she asked, the more frightened I became. Once I assured my mom that I did not hurt myself, she made a sad smile. She began to tell me that I was having my "period". Like I knew what she was talking about. Period? Isn't that some type of punctuation? Mom never mentioned the words "becoming a woman". I was to accept this *curse* because it happens to all girls. She asked me to walk with her to her bedroom. She went to the closet and handed me a triangle shaped elastic band that had two hooks at either end. Then she gave be this big fat white tissue thing. It was called a pad. The next thirty minutes seemed like an eternity. I kept thinking why God did this to girls. He must have been really angry with Eve.

I remember putting out the lounge chair in the front yard, watching all my friends play. I lay there, feeling sorry for myself and all girls who had to experience the *curse*. I wonder why my friends never mentioned, maybe they felt like me. I never knew if my mother told my dad. I kept it to myself for quite some time. Little did I know that I would have the *curse* for the next forty years!

I knew my life was going to be different now. What would become of me? I was not ready for the "boy" thing and I was not ready for "girly" thing either. I felt I was a misfit.

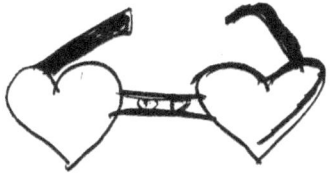

Chapter 2

Becoming of Age

I have become an inexperienced girl. What does that mean? I had no idea where to begin, that is, in becoming girly.

I enjoyed watching my mother put on make-up and those lotions. After all, she was used to me watching her. But I had a plan. I could casually ask her questions about make-up, lotions, shaving, perfumes, and maybe about boys. I just may wait about asking her about boys. At least mom was an expert on make-up.

I wasn't quite ready to make that leap to womanhood. I did not consider myself a woman.

I laid there on the bed as usual, watching mom put on her Avon lotion. I asked her why she puts on so many lotions. She told me that one lotion takes off the foundation, another lotion takes off the eye make-up, another lotion takes off the lipstick, and the final lotion helps remove…. Oh! I don't know if I can say it…wrinkles.

So "Where do wrinkles come from?" I asked. "Well, honey as we get older, we get wrinkles." She did not know that still didn't answer my question. And besides, who was old? And besides that, who wanted to go through all those lotions? Not me!

Girls, I was in a dilemma. What am I going to do? Do I go on with this lotion business or not? Am I starting to like,like boys? Hey, "in those days" this is all I had to worry about.

I wonder if you, the reader experience this same dilemma.

I think my mother pick up on my interest in her daily face routine, because when the Avon lady came, guess who was invited to look at some "girly" stuff? Yep, me.

Of course, they had some neat stuff. I liked the bottles that the different products came in. I remember my mother had quite a collection. The Avon Lady was ready, willing, and able to show me the latest teen products. I was allowed to choose some cologne. I chose not to select any make-up items at the time. I wanted to gradually grow into the girly thing.

One day, it finally hit me..the **boy bug.** You know that bug that bites and tells you it is time to like-like boys. My friends and I were playing in the alley. When this really cute boy came over and introduced himself to us. He seemed nice. He asked if he could join in. We were playing "High and Low", it was a game where we would raise a rope to different heights and jump over it. I was good at this game. We played all afternoon. In fact, he became a regular with us after school.

Then one day, he asked me if he could take me to the movies. I thought he meant all of us go, I found out that is not what he meant.

Well, my friends were so excited for me. I was going on a "date". I never thought of it as a date, just two friends going to the movies. Why was there any pressure about dating?

My parents knew him and his mother. His father had passed away.

His older brother was in his twenties. He was going to be the driver. The movie was a James Bond movie, not that I was into James Bond, I guess because of the peer pressure I was trying to be interested in dating. Everyone was making it out to be such a big deal. I wonder if I am supposed to make it a big deal, because most of my friends were really into boys. I kept wondering if something was wrong with me.

As we entered the theater, you could see the smoke filtered room because of the darkness; it was like a gray cloud hanging in the air. Oh, "in those days", people could smoke in the theaters. My friend found a dark corner to sit. We enjoyed the cartoons, then it was time for the main feature; when suddenly, I felt an arm over my shoulders. As his arm lay upon my shoulders, my heart began beating fast, but why? Was it warm in here or what? Then, it happened, his face connected with my lips. His lips were warm, I was warm. OMG… my friends were right. I was feeling wonderful. I had so many different feelings going on inside. It was a great evening. He paid for everything. I did not have to spend a penny. And I had my first real kiss!

Girls, do you remember your first kiss? I told my girlfriends about the kiss, but I did not tell my parents. I think my mom would have told me that I could get pregnant and my dad probably would have beaten him up. My dad saw me as his little "sugar". I really think he did not want me to grow up, bless his heart.

I found myself thinking about other guys. During this awkward time, I was a little on the heavy side, now it wasn't fat, it was "baby fat", at least that is what my mother told me. It was hard for me to believe that a guy would want to date me.

One day he called. He invited me to his house. No problem, I went over. I noticed his mother and brother were gone, and as a good girl I inquired to their whereabouts. They were "out". He wanted to show me something in his room. No problem, I went into his room, it was very neat and clean. He sat on the bed and he invited me to sit. No problem, I sat. He leaned over and kissed me. Then I felt his hand going where no boy's hand has gone before! I jumped up and told him to stop it! My heart was pounding, was it pounding from the touch or was it pounding because I was afraid?

He wanted me to come back and sit down. I knew I was going to hell, or worse yet, get pregnant. Girls, I told you I was naïve.

I told him I needed to home, and I ran home as fast as I could. I felt like I had sinned. God was going to punish me now. I knew I could not tell my parents, but I told my friends. Girls, you know how that goes. One friend will tell you that is what boys do; the other ones tell you he was after only one thing.

Except, I did not know what that one thing was; I see you chuckling to yourself.

I am telling you the truth! I had no idea. Remember, my mom only told me about the *curse*, nothing else. She would use the word "pregnant" but I did not know how girls got pregnant, and I was sixteen!

I am sure that there are some of you doubters thinking I was sort of dork head. I guess I was. But for some reason, my mother chose not to discuss the "how tos" and the "what nots". I can remember taking a certain class in high school, it was where the girls went to the class; the boys went to another class. The nuns talked about being a "good" girl and looking at becoming a nun. There was never a mention about what not to do with boys. It was a promo for nuns. I wonder if the boys were in a promo for priests.

Little did I know that my life was changing. Time was changing.

Chapter 3

Times are changing

That was the beginning and ending of a first date.

Don't get me wrong I was still interested in boys; the "boy crazy bug" got me, even though I was a late bloomer.

I found myself going to dances every Friday night at the local public school. I really liked to dance, especially slow dancing. I was being a good careful girl.

We had a girls' night at my friend's house. We would order pizza and listening to music, and talk about boys.

One of my friends mentioned that I had thick eyebrows (like I really noticed), and I should consider having them "thinned". She told me my eyes were very blue, but I really could use some eye help. I told her OK. I think that is when I learned that there is good pain and bad pain. This was the good pain because it was going to make my face prettier, according to my friends. I was just a little hesitant because I thought my dad may not approve of this change.

Anyway, I lived through it. Putting ice on the area helped the red, swollen bad pain. My dad never noticed. My friends and I would get together and we would "experiment" on each other. Girls of age, you know what I mean. We would try wearing different make-up, giving each other hairs do's, and wearing fake jewelry. Some of the best times were when we would call boys. Why? It was fun. Of course, if it was a boy we knew and one of us liked, we would take turns asking if he liked so and so.

I found myself spending less and less time with my mother lying on the bed, watching her do the makeup thing. I miss that. I was spending more time with my friends, trying to become a young teen..a girly teen.

One night, I walked into my parent's bedroom and I noticed a pair of glasses on the dresser. My mother came in to do her daily face routine, and I had mentioned the glasses. She told me that her eyes were getting tired and words were becoming blurry. She had gone to a doctor and he recommended glasses, big, round, and blue ones!

She seemed not very happy about it. She told me it wasn't that great getting old. I couldn't believe that she said that, why, she wasn't old, at least not to me. She could never get old. She had beautiful skin. The more I looked at her; I could see those lines around her eyes. Now, you may not want to hear this, if you smoke, but those lines were from her smoking. She started smoking when she was eighteen, now she was in her forties. At that time, age meant nothing to me. I looked forward to birthdays, my mother did not; I couldn't understand that part, just yet.

By this time, I was well into wearing make-up. It still didn't seem fair, that girls had to go through this how ordeal of wearing make-up and doing the lotion thing, while boys, well some boys, shaved. Plus, they did not have the "curse" every month. How did we girls get so lucky?

Time went by as usual, still not concerned about aging, like my mother was. I do remember feeling different about Christmas. I guess part of me wanted to believe that Santa really came but reality was …maybe I better not go there. I believed in the Spirit of Christmas and still do.

One Christmas, I received an ice skating outfit and a pair of beautiful white skates. I was so excited. My parents told me that there was an ice skating rink several miles away that was opening up during the weekend. Dad would take me, and he would return in a few hours. I look back and think those were the only times Dad and I really spent any time with him. He took me and dropped me off. He would return in two and half hours. Bless his heart.

Learning how to skate was not very pleasant. I did not know that a body could sustain so much impact on the cold and wet ice.

But I was determined I would see this to the end, plus there were plenty of good looking guys out there on the ice.

I really enjoyed those times. I taught myself how to skate. I met many new friends, both boys and girls.

By this time, I had lost all that "baby fat", and started to blossom into a young lady. I no longer wore a training bra; it was time for the real McCoy. I noticed boys noticing me.

It was time to start putting on makeup, to look more grown up. My life had changed…I became a makeup junky.

I remember a funny incident one morning. I had become lazy when it came to taking off the makeup. Why take it off? I was going to put it on the next day. I know, really dorky. I woke up the next morning, and I wondered why my pillow was tan…and what was wrong with my face…ugh! Well, you can just imagine what your face would look like…the drool spots, the smeared mascara, and the areas where the foundation was wiped clean away. I learned a lesson that day, always wash your face and remove the makeup. Plus my mother did not appreciate washing a brown pillow.

When the Avon lady came, it was time to purchase face cleaning products. Then it happened, OMG…pimples! How awful! What is next? First, the curse, and then the shaving of armpits, legs, and plucking eyebrows. What would we look like if we did not shave or pluck? now PIMPLES! Girls it just doesn't' seem fair, does it. My friends were experts at pimples. No problem, they would tell me what to do. Although, some friends insisted that those bumps be squeezed, others said to use Clearasil. Say, that product still exists today, doesn't it? Those pimples seem to come at the time as the curse. My friends told me that if I ate chocolate, "you will break out." By this time, I was into the makeup thing. I had thoughts about becoming a beautician, which is what we called a stylist "in those days". My mother let me experiment on her. It was fun. I loved doing her hair. One day she allowed me to put her make up on her, since I was an experienced beautician.

I started with the foundation on her soft skin. I noticed she had "lines". I tried smoothing those lines out from her face, but they kept springing back. I had not noticed those lines before. I asked my mother about those lines. I guess it was not a good thing to ask. She informed me of "age lines". Age lines? Laugh lines? Frown lines? Just how many lines are there? And Crow's feet? How do you get a crow's foot next to your eye? I know what you are thinking, a dork. Obviously, she did not appreciate my discovery of her lines.

Again, getting old never crossed my mind. I had other things to be thinking about… dating, and a certain college guy.

Chapter 4

Falling in Love

Well girls, it happened. I found "the guy".

It was a cool fall Saturday morning. My dad had agreed to take me to the ice skating rink. I had planned to stay for several sessions; sessions were about two and half hours. It was there that I met "him". I was resting after skating a bit, when a young boy came up to me and said, "See that guy over there?" He wants to know if you will skate with him." I said yes. That was the first time I said yes. The second time, was when he asked me to marry him…oh, I guess I am going too far ahead. Sorry, it sounded good, so I decided to put this in at this point in the story.

He was wearing hockey skates, so I knew he had to be a good skater. He introduced himself, and he told me he was going to Indiana University. OMG! a college man. I was only a sophomore in high school. Was this a dream come true or what? I had my ups and downs growing up as a young woman, a native young woman. This dating thing was kind of new, but it was fun. The college man wanted to get serious, just date him exclusively. I wasn't ready for that. But as the years went by; my thoughts of this young man was becoming stronger.

Two years later, I graduated from high school.

I felt lost somehow…I can't really explain it. I wanted to be a teacher, but my parents could not afford to pay for college like most of my friends. There is a reality check when you receive your diploma. You know you have reached an age when you are considered an adult…a time you are expected to go out on your own. I remember having a lump in my stomach. I wondered what if I could have done things differently, too late. I pretended that I was going to Ball State with my friends. I had such an empty feeling, most of my friends were off to college; I had to look for work. This was a time of reflection. Things would have been different.

I found work at a government center. The pay was good and there were plenty of young engineers from Purdue University. I must admit, wearing makeup was "had to do" thing for me. Remember, I was a late bloomer; this dating business was new to me. Yes, I was still dating the college man, but now he was a teacher at a local middle school.

I liked dating different guys. I liked the attention. Yet, my mind kept thinking about "the guy". The guy must have been thinking about me too; because he asked me to marry him, after several years of dating, Of course, I said yes.

I remember waking up my mom around midnight to tell her the news. She was just as excited as I was. We were engaged for a year. I wanted to make sure this was the right guy. It was fun that year looking at gowns, flowers, and the bride to be stuff. It was a good time to enjoy with my mother. I really think my parents were happy. I wondered if they felt I was going to be an Old Maid. In those days, I guess girls were supposed to be thinking about getting married and raising children.

Here was an opportunity for my mother to tell me the "secrets" of marriage. But she did not. Realize I am twenty now. Again, I see you shaking your head and rolling your eyes. Hey this was back in the late sixties people and my family never told me life's secrets.

I really do not want to get into my life as a married woman; this book is not about that. It is about growing up…aging gracefully, or at least trying to. One thing I do remember was when I had gone to a local bar with my new husband. I had ordered a beer. The server asked to see my ID. Are you kidding? I was highly insulted. Oh; those were the good old times. I lost count of the number of times I was carded. And I continued to feel insulted throughout the years.

Time went by quickly.

I remember trying to make ends meet, teachers were not making that much money, and they still don't. We ate Denny Moore Beef Stew; it was in a large can of who knows what, Spam, and a lot of peanut butter sandwiches. I found several jobs that I could handle and go to school at night. I look back on those times. I really amazed myself. I did not think it was hard; we had to survive. Besides I was young and healthy…not worrying about getting older.

My plans to become a teacher had to be put on hold. I was working two jobs. My husband was teaching during the day and working part time at a hardware store; he was also taking a class to work on his Masters. Sound familiar girls? I was working in order to put my husband through school, while my schooling was put aside. We did those things "in those days". Regrets? No, not really. We helped each other out. Marriage is a partnership isn't it? I was so naïve, I saw how my parents worked hard to provide a good life for us. We weren't rich…we weren't poor either.

One of the many jobs I had was being a life guard. Remember? I was the athlete. I loved being outside, the swimming, and the sun. I had long auburn hair; with my sky blue eyes…I looked pretty good for a young married woman. I did not have to wear makeup. Why bother? My skin was a beautiful tan. "In those days" we used iodine and baby oil to help bake ourselves. There wasn't that concern of the

UV rays damaging our skin. It was cool to be like a California girl. I had gone shopping one afternoon, and a young girl approached me and told me that I looked like Ali McGraw. Do you remember the actress? She was Steve McQueen's girlfriend. Why thank you very much!

Now, at this point if you are asking yourself who is Steve McQueen then you are too young to be reading this book. You were warned about the age thing, weren't you?

It was a fun time back in the early seventies.

I look back now, and realize my parents did not do "fun" things anymore, or what I consider fun things. I don't know or remember if they were tired or just preferred to stay at home.

The truth was probably, they were getting older…I did not want to think about it. None of us really do.

Chapter 5

A New Life

Our life was about to change…

We had been married for about five years. I had a good part time job as a model…yes, a model. I worked at a clothing store during the day; and at night I modeled clothes for a private company. Needless to say, it was fun. I do remember having long hair that reached my waist. In order to be hired, I had to have my hair cut to chin length, you want to know why? I was told I looked sixteen! I needed to look older. How sweet!

My husband was teaching at a new junior high school. He taught during the day and still work part time at night. We rarely saw each other. Hey, we were young then. Besides, we really did not have much of a social life. We were too busy trying to save and survive.

In 1975, my husband had accepted a teaching position overseas in West Germany. "In those days" it was called West Germany. We were both very excited. What an opportunity to go on an adventure.

We were in our mid twenties and ready for a new adventure to another part of the world. It was my first time on an airplane. It was a long flight. I was scared to death.

We landed in Frankfurt, West Germany; tired and overwhelmed. These people spoke another language, I couldn't read anything. Going to the bathroom was an experience in itself.. Do you believe it…paying to potty? The toilet paper was like waxed paper. Ever tried it? We were hustled on a bus which would eventually take us to our new temporary quarters. That is military talk. In other words an apartment.

I can say our life was great; it was difficult at times, but we learned to be adventurous and to appreciate being Americans; serving our military families as educators. The military and the many teacher friends we met became our family. The support system for us was wonderful; we were blessed many times over. Living in Germany, I learned to enjoy the festivities, including beer and the wine. They didn't check ID's.

I remember one weekend, a group of teachers decided to go the Munich for the Oktober Fest. Our friends had devised a plan to "borrow" a Munich beer mug. They were considered a rare item. The plan was for me and a Major friend to wait outside the Gasthaus for the "pass" of the mug.

We were in an alley, when a man approached the Major. He spoke German, My friend began to laugh and spoke back to the man in German. The man left, of course, I was curious. Anyway, the man thought I was a prostitute. It was very common in certain areas of Germany. I found no comfort in knowing that. Well, you know! I was a young, pretty woman, remember I told you.

We did not seem to have many worries. Sometimes the PX would run out of certain products; we would just go on the economy.

My husband was an excellent teacher. The community loved him. We both were very involved in making the best of what we had. We enjoyed traveling with the ski club. It was cheap, and it was a way to meet new people and see new sights. Germany was absolutely beautiful. We didn't seem to have any cares.

Then..

One day, I noticed I had not had the "*curse*". Odd? For me it was, "odd". I made an appointment with the military doctor. I was told some news that would change our life forever.

You guessed it. I was pregnant. We had not planned on a baby. We had talked about it, but we were not ready. I went from a size one to extra large. I was twenty five years old. I had morning, noon, and night sickness. The baby was due in July. My husband was somewhat shocked, like how did this happen! We weren't ready, too late now...I was healthy and pregnant. My pregnancy did not slow me down too much. We were able to do some traveling, as long as there was a bathroom nearby. We even joined the ski club. I learned to ski in Bavaria, Germany.

I kept on blossoming, until I could no longer see my feet.

Our daughter was born in July of 1976, the year of the bicentennial. It was not as easy as it sounds. The birthing was easy; the pains were not so good. I remember waiting in the room for the nurse to bring our baby to me. I waited and waited. Finally, the doctor came in. He began asking me how old I was. What has that to do with anything? Where was my baby? My stomach began to feel queasy. I felt there was something the doctor wasn't telling me.

He hesitated several times. He told me that our daughter had Downs...I did not know what he was talking about. He continued to tell me the best thing would not see her and put her in an institution. What in the heck was he talking about? Honestly, it is like it happened yesterday. I never heard of Down 's syndrome before.

I felt a lump in my stomach. Why was he asking about my age? What has that to do with my baby? It seemed like I waited forever for my husband to visit; maybe he could make sense of this.

When he arrived; I sounded like a hysterical woman, I probably was. As I began to tell my husband, his face turned pale. I knew then, it was not good news concerning our baby girl. He told me that our daughter would be retarded. I think I must have blocked that part out; because I remember calling for the nurse to bring me my baby. After becoming a pest, the nurse finally brought in our beautiful little girl. She looked fine to me. Maybe the doctors made a mistake.

"In those days", there was a myth that women who were in their late thirties had a higher risk of having a Downs baby; so much for their myth. The doctor called it a "fluke". Fluke or not, our daughter was going home with us, despite what the doctor wanted us to do… put her away in an institution!

I heard so much information about Downs's people from friends and neighbors; it seemed that they were all experts in raising a Downs child. The information they thought they knew, was not good information; in fact it was quite depressing. People would stare at Jennifer and made snide remarks about my age. Ignorant people think that only women in their late thirties and forties had such babies. Soon I learned that age does not matter in the condition of a baby.

Our daughter has grown up in a better world than what those doctors had wanted for her. I met many ignorant people who were raised to believe a stereotypical way about Down's people. These same people continue to raise their children with those same terrible beliefs. Jennifer is one of the reasons why I am a great teacher…she is the blossom on my tree. Jennifer has touched many people in her life. She has helped me believe that anything is possible; and age is just a word that seems to make some people act a certain way.

Life is taking one day at a time; take a deep breath and thank the Lord for His blessings.

We had another blessing …

We had a son a few years after Jennifer was born. It was a little scary, that is getting pregnant again. I put my faith in the Lord. Our son was fine in every way, although he looked like Mr. Spock when he was born. It is interesting to note, the doctor never asked me about how old I was.

Our children thrived in the many places we lived. We took advantage of traveling to different countries and learning about different cultures. I stayed home for several years to work with Jennifer and enjoy Jason's curiosity. Maybe deep down inside I want to protect Jennifer from a cruel world.

When I felt that Jennifer and I were ready for a change. I decided to go back to work. It was time to go back to work. I was able to find teaching assistant positions, but the desire to be a teacher was very strong. I was not going to give up my dream, even if I was in my late thirties.

As with any marriage, we had our ups and downs. Midlife crisis as I was told. I won't go into detail…I became a stronger woman during some difficult times.

Our life was about to change again. My husband accepted a principal's job in Misawa, Japan. The average snow fall is around 360 inches. I loved the snow, but I wasn't quite sure about the change in culture. Our German neighbors could not believe we would go to such a place.

Hey, we were still young and adventurous.

Chapter 6

Times of joy and sadness

The year is 1987; we are living in Misawa, Japan. My husband is now a principal of a high school. I have decided it is my time to go back to school. I hope you are telling me, "It's about time".

I remember being very excited…just like a school girl. I meant to say, I really never liked school, so I can imagine what it must have felt like for those kids who couldn't wait for school to start. I signed up for three classes. I looked back and think, I must have been crazy. I was a mom, wife, substitute teacher, volunteered at my children's school, and now a full time student. I walked into my psychology class and froze. I do not know what I was thinking. All of the other students were younger than I was. Then it hit me. I was older. I also felt intimidated. It is now or never, I told myself. Fortunately, I met a woman who was about three years younger, we hit it off right away. The scariest part was taking college algebra. Math was not my forte'. But it was a requirement from the University. I spent many, many hours studying and practicing equations. My husband helped me but I have to admit I was embarrassed that I had to ask for his help. Now I know why teachers want you to pay attention in class. I would think of all kinds of excuses…being older than everyone…I was stressed. Lucky for me I had a understanding and patient professor. He could tell I was stressed and having difficulty with some of the sections of math. He helped me before and after class. He arranged for another student to help me. It just so happened that her husband was a teacher at my husband's school. I manage to earn a B. School became easier and easier. I think my friend and I were more "mature" than the other students. We had experience. Now, doesn't that sound better than saying, we were "old hags".

Again, we had great times in Misawa, Japan; but now my husband's job has taken us to Okinawa, Japan after three years living in Misawa. This was our sixth move. We did not look at it as a bad thing, it was a new adventure. Our children were very flexible and they had friends in Europe and Japan.

I never slowed down. I kept up with my university classes in Okinawa. In some cases, I was not the oldest in class. Age was never an issue with any professors or other students.

It was during this time I was able to earn my BS degree. I was ready to fulfill my dream. I could not have done it without the help of my family and friends. The classes had to meet the requirements of the University and the Department of Defense Schools. My family was very supportive of my dream. I am in my forties by now…early forties. So girls, if I could do it so can you. It was hard at times. But I managed; I would get up around three a.m. to study for about four hours. Then I would get the children up, fix breakfast, and take them to school, and I would head for the library or class.

I don't recall thinking about getting older, or even my age back then. It wasn't a concern…or worry.

By this time, our children were teenagers. This was the hard part for me. I realized that they were growing up. The teen years were not as bad as some people say they were. Our children grew up overseas, not in America. We did make trips back to the states during most summers.

I wanted to see my parents, and our children to learn to know their grandparents. We would visit every two years. It was becoming very obvious to me that my parents were aging. I could see more gray hairs; dad was moving a lot slower. He had a chair that would lift him up so he could get out of the chair easier. They chose not to go sightseeing with us. I would think, "Where did the time go?"

We were always anxious to get back home in Okinawa, home was not just a fixture or where our things were; it was where our hearts belonged. Secretly maybe I did not want to see my parents getting older; out of sight, out of mind.

I want you to know my dream came true in May of 1992. I graduated with a 3.6 GPA, not bad for an old lady. That August I was offered a teaching position at one of the elementary schools. I made it! Anything is possible. Teaching felt so natural. My mom told me that I had a gift; God has blessed me with an overabundance of love. Needless to say, my family was very proud. I look back on those days…years, and I still can't believe I did it.

It was a wonderful six years… a fast six years. My husband and I realized that our son would be going to college, far, far away…in America. Now that was scary. We had read in the Stars and Stripes the number of gangs in high schools…the crime. Our son was not thrilled.

We have not had any practice being "Americans" for over twenty plus years. When the opportunity came around for my husband to obtain a job in the United States, he did. His job was going to be in Washington, DC. What a place…for newbies. I remember living in a hotel for a few weeks..not fun, except for the TV commercials. We had rented a temporary house in McLean, Virginia. I had to call and make an arrangement for a phone to be connected. I dialed, and then there was this lady who sounded like a robot who kept giving all of these choices. "If you want…press 1; if you want…press 2. Boy, she was speaking so fast. I began to cry and threw the phone across the room. It was called voice mail. I knew then we were in America, but it wasn't the America we had left twenty three years ago. We were living in the FAST LANE! It was very obvious that we were not ready for America's new way of life…new for us.

I did not have time to worry about my, age; I was busy worry about surviving. Driving, well…let's not go there. Give me the autobahns in Germany.

After several weeks, we began looking for a house to buy. This was my job. My husband had a great boss who arranged for a realtor to pick me up and go house hunting. We found a nice house in a quiet neighborhood. In fact, one of our neighbors was a naval officer.. someone who we could relate to.

And this is where it all began…

Of course, I wouldn't known it…NOT..for some reason I started receiving letters for AARP, Social Security, and senior discount coupons. I had to check the envelope again to make sure it was my name on the envelope, no, it was not a mistake. It should have had my husband's name on it. What is going on? How is this possible? Is there someone with a huge data base system who is watching files on people who are close to turning fifty? I mean…how did they know? And I still wonder how they know. Not only do I still receive AARP info, I am receiving "Senior Living" information. Maybe there are "spies".

I was not a happy person. My husband just laughed. Was I supposed to feeling a certain way? Like old? I was in my prime, people! I was healthy and active. But reading those flyers, it sounded like I was ready for the old folk's home. I dare any of those people to find a gray hair on my head. Luckily, the angry feeling left, I had other things to worry about. I wanted to find a teaching position. I put in my application in several schools. At that time, it never occurred to me that my age could be a factor in being hired. Most teachers my age were thinking about their retirement in ten years. I was just starting a teaching career in America. I was starting to feel sorry for myself when I received a phone call from a school. It was about a ten minute drive. I was offered to teach third grade Language Arts and Social Studies part time. I took it. The hardest part of the job, was learning the culture, it wasn't the teaching. I was the new kid.. ha… near fifty year old kid who hasn't lived in the US for twenty something years.

My teaching style is very different from the way most teachers taught. I march to a different drummer. It could have been that I love what I do. Children are very perceptive. As with any teaching job, I was having fun, despite some of the negative looks I would receive. Remember early, I had mentioned being a rebel. I believe these people had judged me by my age…like I should not be acting like I am having fun. Maybe it was the way I dressed, or how my room was arranged with flashing lights. Who knows? Teaching kept me feeling alive! (And it still does)

 I wonder if there was a secret or color coded icon that was invisible to me but I could swear that the postman loved delivering those letters from those agencies that kept telling me I was getting ready to kick the bucket or put out to pasture.

One day I was driving home from school and I began to feel very sleepy. I could not stay awake. I made sure the air conditioning was on full blast. I turned up the radio. I remember making it upstairs and laying on the bed. My husband woke me up several hours later. I still was so sleepy. I found myself getting tired and I never seem to be able to get enough sleep. I guess it was time to see a doctor. I chose a female doctor. Someone I could relate with…male doctors had a tendency to tell me how old I was…and blah..blah. My mother warned me about them. No offense to male doctors. The doctor wanted to do some tests. It turned out that I have thyroid condition. It seems my mother had the same condition. No problem, just take the medicine.

Life at school was still my joy. Jennifer was attending a great high school. They were able to meet her needs. I just did not like the long bus drive. Jason was trying to enjoy his life in high school too. We did feel bad about taking him out of school during his junior year back in Okinawa. He was highly insulted when the school

made him take the sixth grade competency test, it was required…
we couldn't say…but it was ridiculous. His high school transcripts
showed he had earned all A's and B's.

I was offered a full time teaching position the next year. I was
winning over some of the other teachers. For some reason, the
students and teachers started calling me Miss Frizzle from The Magic
School Bus series. I guess there was some connection. Although, I
would never wear a dress with bugs on it..maybe the shoes.

It did not take long for us to realize that our life overseas was a lot
easier than it is living in America. We had no time to have fun. Life
was on that fast track. Our house was our recluse. It took work to
make it "our" home but it was a great place to live.

THEN…

One morning I woke up with severe stomach pains. I knew what
time it was…time for the *curse* again. The pain was terrible. I could
barely walk. Yes, it was time. I was miserable for several days. But
the *Curse* did not go away. I was beginning to worry. What was
happening to me? I did not tell anyone. I was too afraid. Gee,
this sounds familiar; I knew I had to see the doctor. The *curse* had
lasted nearly two weeks. Something wasn't right. I waited anxiously
in the doctor's office, looking at all of those pamphlets that discuss
diseases and "conditions"; which I knew I had to have a conditions.
The doctor did her examination. She told me I needed to have a
D and C, which meant "light surgery". Of course, I panic. Who
wouldn't? She continued. I was told that I might me going through
"the change". You know that word girls: MENOPAUSE. Well, I was
PRE-menopausal, like it mattered. Say, why is it called MENopause?
It has nothing to do with MEN. Why isn't called WOMENPAUSE?
Haven't you ever wondered why it is called MENopause?

The doctor asked me if I had experienced hot flashes, night sweats,
or mood swings. I told her no. Gee, here I am again, supposed to be
going through this change, and I am not doing it right. All I knew
was that the *curse* would be gone…gone for good! I could handle

this. She prescribed an estrogen pill. I guess so I won't grow a hump, grow whiskers, or "dry" up and wither away. It turns out that several years later; I had a blood clot on my lung. God was watching out for me. As you guessed, I was taken off estrogen. Now, what was going to happen to me? Grow a beard? My voice becomes deeper? Grow a certain male body part? OMG!

Believe it or not, I did not have the wrinkles that society thinks that most almost half a century women are supposed to have. Teaching kept me young, my students kept me young. It was nice to hear them call me "mom".

This was also a time for a "reality check". Everything was going great at home, Still we did not seem to have fun like we used to. We were able to talk weekly with my parents, that was a plus. We talked weekly. I could tell that something was going on by mom's voice. She would always keep bad situations from me. She didn't want me to worry. One night I received a phone call from my mom. My dad had heart surgery, prognosis was good but my dad had developed a staph infection. Mom wanted me to come immediately. I was on the next flight to Indianapolis. My brother and sister in law picked me up. I felt they were keeping something from me. It was good to see mom again, although she looked a lot older to me. She had never looked so old before. It was kind of scary. I wanted to go to hospital right away. Mom did her best to comfort me…to prepare me. Wait a minute; I don't understand what is going on. Dad was doing fine a few days ago. What has changed?

I held onto mom's hand. I did not like the feeling of this hospital floor. It was the IC room. I walked into dad's room. It did not even look like him…like who I remembered. What became of that tall handsome of a man. This man was frail. Tubes were coming out from everywhere. I could barely swallow. I went over to his side. The nurses told me he was unconscious and he would not know that I am there. The machine was keeping him alive. Those terrible sounds of the heart monitor and the pumping of the respirator were endless.

I touched his beautiful silver hair and called his name. I kissed his cheek. It was as if my touch brought him back for a split second. He sat up with his arms outstretched and then he laid back down. My heart pounded. I told the nurse he knew I was here. Of course, she disregarded it. But I knew...he waited for me to come...for me to say good-bye. The doctor asked to see us outside the room. He told mom what most family members do not want to hear. We left. It wasn't but an hour and we received the call...dad had passed.

We did our best to prepare for the night. We wept. It wasn't until later that my brother told me the day he walked side by side with dad into the surgery room a week ago; dad told my brother to tell me "good-bye". My dad did not want to go on living the way he had been..frail and always a worry to mom, especially when the doctors told him to no longer drive. He felt he would never be well again. It seems that if my dad had survived the surgery and the recovery; there was a plan to take out an artery from his neck and replace it with an artery from his leg. Dad had diabetes. Some of his toes were already black, which meant those would have to be removed. My dad did not want to go through it. He was tired... very tired.

 His death was the reality check for me. Time had passed me by. just once why couldn't I stop time...just a little. My dad was eighty three years old. He did not look old in my eyes, but he was old in everyone else's eyes. I think I aged that week I spent with my mom. It was very difficult going through dad's things. Luckily, mom and dad had made arrangements, but it still was hard to do. My husband and I wanted my mom to come live with us but she felt she could not leave dad, her home, and her friends. Hardly did I realize my life was going to change dramatically.

Another adventure and another reality check.

It was time...time for another adventure. My husband was offered another position. Another move, here I go again. We moved to Beaufort, South Carolina. I had to learn a whole new culture. I pictured myself on the veranda sipping sweet tea. Yeah, right. Our house was on an island,...sounds cool doesn't it? It was a nice area with hundred year old oak trees with the Spanish moss hanging down. It was a very quiet neighborhood. If you were lucky, you would spot a neighbor every now and then.

This was the time I turned the big 50...half a century. Yes, I was fifty. Many people were surprised that I was fifty. They thought I was a lot younger. OK, I will take the compliments but I have nothing to hide. Although I noticed I was getting a little plumper. Some body parts began to sag just a little. Still no problem, I found a good secret..Victoria Secret. So far, she is the only one who knew my secret.

I wanted to continue with teaching. For a spit second I wondered if schools were hiring fifty year old women. Never considered myself old; I love to teach. My son told me one time that I had a certain "magic" that children see. We could be sitting in a restaurant and a child would be at another table, then all of sudden the child would look at me and wave. My husband would ask if I knew the child. I would tell him, no. I really can't explain it...it something special God has given me.

Soon..

I was blessed. I had an interview and I was hired to teach kindergarten. Now, if anyone can teach kindergarten...you have to be young at heart, mind, and body. Those little ones keep you on your toes. It was also a time I was sick a lot. Which meant seeing a new male doctor who would remind me of how old I was..blah..blah..blah. was brutal to me.

I continued to get my AARP information, as well as the latest on assisted living facilities. I know there is a data base out there. How did it know we moved from Virginia to South Carolina? Makes you wonder doesn't it? I found myself watching women my age, what was the one thing in common? Hair. I noticed that most of the fiftyish women wore short hair. So, if you are fiftyish or older, do you have short hair? I started to notice more fiftyish women, why?

Was I really fifty? I did not act like any of them…really. My inner strength was much younger than my body..I guess. Although, when you think about it, my innards are old too. You know what I mean. Think of what a prune looks like. It is wrinkly on the outside, but it is good for you. Do you get it? Oh well, I decided I would rebel… yes…I would rebel. I would let my hair grow long. I tried it. I had extensions put in my hair. I know what you are thinking right now. Yep.. Not a good idea. I looked like a frump. I would exercise more…yeah. But first, I had to find another teaching position at fifty years old.

Again, I was blessed. I think God's plan for me was not finished. My mom believed God had given me a gift. I believed it too. I continue believe that most teachers are very special people. Unless you have walked in our shoes…you have no idea what our job entails.

I had become a Kindergarten teacher. It was wiping noses, tying shoes, zipping zippers, and teaching them how to flush a toilet. The school was located in an older neighborhood. I would have never guessed that there were so many school aged children in that neighborhood. Being a Kindergarten teacher is not for the young at heart. It is for the fittest and bravest teachers only. I learned a great deal from them, And I know I learned that a five year old is capable of doing anything you want them to do. This is where the rebel in me ventured out. For some reason, the system did not believe that five and six year olds could not read or compute math. It was forbidden to teach them to read. OMG, once you teach them the letters and sounds…guess what happens next? DUH…reading. I wondered if the school board decided to hire me because they thought I was from the "old" school of thinking. HA, little did they know what they were getting. Remember, the doctors told me that Jennifer would not be able to read, write, walk,blah…blah. I knew that the majority of these children could more than just color, cut, and paste. It is whatever your expectations are. I enjoyed teaching Kindergarten and it was time to try something new. My principal asked if I would loop; it means I would move up with my students to first grade. I liked this idea.

I remember one of the fiftyish aged teachers would make remarks concerning how I would dress. She would not mix any words telling me she didn't like what I wore. I told her she probably wouldn't like my thong either. I wondered if she ever smiled. After a few years, she began to soften a little. One day I wore a cute jean Capri outfit. She told me, normally she does not like what I wore, but today she liked it. I guess that meant I was accepted.

Teaching first graders was fun. It kept me busy; most of them knew how to flush a toilet and tie shoes. It will be an easy year.

I have noticed that there are some older folks who have no patience... like five year olds. I am sure you have seen/heard them in stores and restaurants. It's like they throw tantrums. There was a lady in her late seventies...gee, she just about ran me over so she could get in front of me at the checkout. The reason why I mentioned it, my mom and dad would expect to be seated right away at a restaurant; and the hostess to serve coffee immediately. You really can't say it is age related remember little kids do the same thing. Ponder that.

Mom came to visit one summer. It was nice to be with her again. She tried to be active, but she was just so tired. I had that terrible feeling in my stomach. I realized I was fifty and she was in her late seventies. I guess I was old...a half a century old. And mom seemed to have aged so quickly. She had a hard time walking. She was always out of breath. She told me she had a slight case of emphysema. I wondered how a person can have a slight case of it. It is times like this that I find it hard that she is gone, I miss her so much. I thought I could write about that part of my life but as I reminisce; honestly, I can't do it..She was my very best friend. I love you, mom. Mom, I thought you would live forever. You are always in my heart.

Ever since her death..

My life had changed. I found myself looking at the obituaries... especially the ages of the people who died. I know it sounds creepy. Now, with my mom gone...I felt vulnerable. I look at life differently. There are some People who take life for granted. There is this feeling of entitlement. I see it in some of my students, their parents, and other people.

I had an appointment to have a mammogram at the hospital. As I walked down the hallway, there lying in bed outside the X-ray room, was an elderly woman. She looked pale, frail, and lonely. I smiled. She managed a small smile. People were walking past her, like she wasn't even there. I was on the brink of tears. No one to talk to her, to reassure her everything would be fine; she was abandoned. It could be me or you some day. She is someone's wife, mother, sister, or a friend. How soon we forget.

In other cultures, the elderly live with the family. They look after one another. They are respected for their experience and what they have shared with the family. In our culture, we seem to want to get away from out parents and to look after ourselves. Some people frown or make fun of adults who live with their parents.

The economy has forced many adults to move back with their parents; bringing their own children. I wonder how many parents turn away their adult children. Isn't it about family...love?

Life Sucks at times.

Chapter 7

Just Hang in There (easier said than done)

Remember being young and you just couldn't wait for your birthday? I would look forward to marble cake, chocolate ice cream, and presents. My mother told me that she had a "debutant" sixteenth birthday. I was too much of a tomboy; just give me money. It seems that after our sixteenth birthday; we look forward to being eighteen and on our own. Well, some of us weren't ready to be on our own. At twenty-one, most of my friends were out of college. After twenty-one, do we stop counting birthdays? Some people seem to dread the leap from twenty-one to thirty. I wasn't bothered by birthdays. Mom would always want us to forget her birthday, like if we don't celebrate; it will stop time. Maybe mom and other people realize that they are one year older than last year. The clock is ticking.

You have heard of the saying that as you get older, everything begins to hang. At first, I wasn't a believer, now...well girls it is true for some of us. If you are an athlete and maintain a body of a twenty year old, please read pass this paragraph. This does not pertain to you.

I would have thought my boobs would have stayed the same. After all I really never was endowed. It is just amazing how they hang, what happened to the perkiness? But I fixed that problem with VS...Victoria Secret. She has many secrets. With her help, I am no longer hanging in there...I am "perky". Of course, some my friends are talking about having a "boob job". I don't think I want to go through all that. Besides, I would have to undergo a whole transformation. I think the only thing that would not have to be "fixed" would be my hair. It is all I could afford.

I recently had a mammogram. I overheard the technician tell a nursing student that you tell the difference between older looking breasts than younger looking breasts. Well, I could too. Which one hangs and which one doesn't. This is true, but older looking breasts have more fibrous material inside than a younger breast. Then I pondered...what about those women who have breasts implants. Do they take it out? This sounds like checking the age of horses. You look at their teeth. Hearing that discussion made me feel old; it is probably true. I felt it was another tick mark for me.

As I had mentioned early, I have always been active, especially through exercising. I joined a local "girls" club. It was fun at first. Then I started to notice...where were the young girls? The average age of the club had to have been fifty. These ladies were very nice but they talked about their grandchildren and great grandchildren. I thought ....hum is this what getting older means? I felt I needed a change...maybe I was running away from getting older. I wanted to lose weight and tone up; cause without VS I was just hanging it all out. My doctor recommended a vitamin B shot for energy. Believe it or not girls, I really wasn't hungry. I had to make myself eat.

I decided to use a local program which was approved by my doctor. I had to count calories. The doctor there told me that my body was in a starvation mode; that is why I could not lose weight. Once she put me on the right track I lost close to thirty pounds. Now, guess where all that extra skin went? IT DID NOT GO ANYWHERE...

but down. Have you ever heard of the saggy baggy elephant?…that was me. What was I going to do? Well yeah, I could spend a fortune having a body lift…but girls I am a teacher. Teachers don't make enough money for body lifts, the only thing I could afford would be a tire lift/change. My doctor suggested a new gym and maybe I could hire a personal trainer. Whoa…sounds interesting. I find it amazing how doctors make suggestions to teachers, "go home and rest for about a week"…yeah right or "get a personal trainer". You look around to see if the doctor is really talking to you..a teacher who spends more on her students than herself. But I thought I would try. So I went over to the gym and inquired about joining the club and the slight possibility of hiring a trainer. It turns out it was reasonable and teachers were given a discounts. We can use any help the public is willing to give.

OMG…I walked into the gym. There were young and old people… pumped. This was my kind of place. I pretended I knew what I was doing, not wanting to look foolish. You have seen it before girls, men with big bellies who see a good looking girl; they suck in their belly, looking all macho. Well, I wanted to look "athletic". I stepped on the elliptical machine; I looked around to make sure no one was watching. I began to elipt..it was hard, my legs and thighs ached. I glanced at the other people who were using the machine…like it was their friend. I chickened out and went to the treadmill….more my style. I did not realize how out of shape I was until that day. I received a phone call a few days later from my personal trainer. He sounded nice. We decided on a time to meet. It was summer time, so I was free most days. I will call him Hans…I like that name. Hans was about twenty two and he was nothing but muscle. He asked me some questions…like what are you willing to do to get in shape? Hans started me out doing easy stretches and exercise. I began to feel very different about myself. I was PUMPED up! I was determined to change that loose skin into muscle. I spent that entire summer getting in shape. Of course, we tell ourselves that once school starts we will make sure we come to the gym at least two to three times a week…Yeah right!

I guess there are teachers out there who can manage their time better than me. I just couldn't find the time. I felt like I was betraying myself. But I just had no time. My mornings start a four thirty and I would get home around five; to take care of the dogs and start dinner. Yes, I have a husband but he would not get home until later. After dinner, I had school work to do. Then bed time for me was eight o'clock. Weekends were spent cleaning house and doing school work (they still are). I have purchased weights and a balancing ball to try to keep up with the toning and balancing for this "old" body of mine. I dust them off every now and then. As you can see by my voice in my writing, I am feeling sorry for myself.

I have looked in the mirror and saw a tired woman, who could use a face lift..I guess I didn't mention about the face falling down. It does girls. I am so gullible. I have purchased every product out there to get rid of those "fine" lines, sags, and wrinkles. I did not have them when I was fat. So what's wrong with this picture?

I suspect that with all the money I spent on face creams, I could have had a face lift and maybe one boob lifted. I even heard that Preparation H tightens your skin. Honey, I ain't putting cream that goes on a butt…on my face.

My husband is older than I am. Does he have to use creams? Ahhh.. NO. He has no wrinkles. SO what is it with men's skin? My dad did not have wrinkles either. I started to notice a few hairs on my chin. Say, what is with this? Am I becoming a man? Will my voice change too? I have noticed some women that have chin hairs…lots; like five o'clock shadows. Now, I have to shave my legs, underarms, and chin. It keeps getting better girls.

I have noticed my husband's legs have no hair. Where did it go? Have you ever wondered why the insides of men's ears get hairy and their eyebrows? I wonder if the hair hormones go from the legs to the ears and eyebrows.

Then the ultimate, I wondered since women's boobs hang, if men's balls hang. I know some of you are blushing. But some friends of mine were having an adult discussion about women and the aging process. Then we thought about men and certain body parts "hanging". We wondered since women can get a "boob" job; if men can get a "ball" job. Also, men can take a pill to keep it up. What do we take? We have hot flashes, night sweats, and mood swings. When was the last time you saw a commercial showing a man experiencing mood swings?

Girls, just hang in there, like me using my VS.

I pretend that I have had a face lift. It is called look in the mirror and pull back the sagging skin on your neck. I wish I could hold it longer than a few minutes; but I think people would stare at me, don't you.

Chapter 8

Do Overs

I am sure that most of us have had an opportunity to rethink our life decisions. I know that I have.

Just what would you "do over?" Make a list. Then think about all the people you have touched in way or another. In some cases, I imagine that some of you would be better off having a "do over".

I feel that certain people have touched me in some way, like our daughter Jennifer. I certainly would not have changed anything that has to do with Jennifer in our life.

I would have liked to have had an opportunity to do research on a Downs child. I think I could have prevented some weight issues with Jennifer. This is a possible do over.

Jennifer has always lived with us. She is our daughter. Some parents of special needs adults have their adult child put in a home. We just couldn't do it. I wonder if we are making the right decision. What if something happens to us? Where would Jennifer go? Who would take care of her? She would be so scared.

Another do over would be, I would have told my parents I love you more. And thanks for doing such a good job of raising me. I would have persisted more to mom to come live with us. I think her life would have been somewhat a little less lonely.

Our life overseas was wonderful...and adventurous. I would not do over that. I even think what we had not moved overseas. I would have been a teacher in a different time and world. But the fact remains; I was touched by the many military children and their families. I have some inspirational colleagues. I would not do over that.

I can honestly say, I wish I hadn't been so fugal. For some reason, we were able to save money overseas, but back in the states...Something changes...changed us. We had to have whatever was popular. We like kids in a toy store. I would definitely do over this.

I think about my parents. They knew how to save. They did not want to keep up with the Jones's. They were happy and content knowing they had each other until it was time for them to depart this world.

 So if you are reading this, make sure you have planned for the future. Time has flown by in my human years. It will for you. Age does not seem to be a worry when we are young and busy with our own lives. We did not think about the future, we thought about the now.

For me, my legacy...I would hope those who knew me; will remember I loved to teach; a child advocate; a fun person to be around, and I enjoyed marching to a different drummer.

And maybe this book won't make it to the top ten or the top fifty; but I hope it brings to you fond memories of times lost, loved ones gone but not forgotten and don't forget how important laughter is in our life. I am forever grateful to those who brought laughter and love to my life.

So what legacy will you leave behind? How do you want to be remembered? The reason I asked those questions, is to cause you to think about your life right now. You can have the biggest house, will people remember you? You can afford a body makeover. Will people remember you? Well…probably. You looked old and fat, and now you look great. You are supposed to chuckle at this point.

By the way, I still have short hair. The truth..it is still hard to look in the mirror and see the dark circles around my eyes, the new wrinkles that seem to come from nowhere, and hear the creaking in my joints. I realized that God made me, but I don't think He would mind if I do a little of refurbishing on his masterpiece. .

You are as young or as old as you feel. And don't let anyone tell you differently. Being a senior has its perks. Enjoy life and each other.

Andrea Heitzman

www.ingramcontent.com/pod-product-compliance
Lightning Source LLC
Chambersburg PA
CBHW061218280526
45784CB00006B/2533